# GRAB YOUR VICTORY HOUR

Learn techniques of 60 minutes morning rituals that will transform you to an extraordinary person. You will be more productive at work and you will achieve great success in life.

GYAN S NARAYAN

**Your Free Gift**

As a token of my thanks for taking out time to read my book, I would like to offer you a free gift:

Visit Kindle store and download your **FREE GIFT**

Acquaint yourself with a time breakup of 60 minutes of morning rituals that will:

1. Completely Transform yourself
2. Bring good health
3. Make you wealthy
4. Make you happy
5. Bring concentration power
6. Bring calmness within you
7. Develop book reading habit
8. Plan your day

Dedicated to all my readers who are committed to waking up early in the morning and making this world a better place to live by becoming better human beings.

I0705310

"Grab Your Victory Hour" talks about the morning rituals you need to perform for 60 minutes after you wake up to charge yourself for the day. Morning hours are the prime time to energize and get the most output for yourself. Various techniques have been discussed in the book, giving you specific time-bound rituals for one hour, which on performing will lead you to become an extraordinary person. Every victory morning ritual talked about in this book, if followed diligently, will make you a guaranteed changed personality. You can gain anything in your life. You can achieve your dreams, become a billionaire, have the best of health and the best of happiness in the world. Whatever position you are at present in your life as a student, homemaker, professional, businessman, sportsperson etc., you are bound to change your personality and will have a positive outlook on life.

Happy Reading!

# Table of contents

# Chapter 1: Introduction

**"Every morning, you have two choices: Continue to sleep with your dreams or wake up and chase them."**

**-Carmelo Anthony**

The sweetest and most joyful period of a lifetime is childhood. Reminiscing on my childhood days with my elder brother who was two years older than me, we were forced to wake up at 4:30 A.M to memorize the subjects taught in the school. My father used an antique alarm clock to wake both of us up. At that time, we were in preschool. Gradually we grew with this morning routine of waking up early. As time went by, our college days began and now we are both working professionals. My elder brother is currently not a morning person, but I have maintained the habit of waking up in the morning. I appreciate the habit of waking up early imbibed in me.

Every parent desire to make their kids shine and get the best results in class and above that, rank first place in school. At that time, I found that I was forced to wake up, but then there was no clarity in my mind about what I was reading and what was getting inside my head. Instead, I would feel sleepy and maybe after a lapse of 45 minutes, my brain and mind would open and I could now read the chapters.

Some research says that morning is the best time for cramming and my father agreed with this. However, I also found that this sentence also has another meaning for my father. My father made doubly sure that we had not slept back and that we were busy reading the books. The sound of our cramming might have given him a sense of fulfilment that kids are learning and their morning hours are best utilized. My brother and I kept on realizing that we were only gainfully utilizing only one of the two hours from 4.30 A.M. to 6.30 A.M. for study, but we dare not say this to our father as he was a strict disciplinarian. This concept of waking up early in the morning led me to research on utilizing the morning's best waking hours. Everyone desires to dream big and achieve their goals like wealth, peak of their career, wisdom, etc. And so was my dream. But the question is how many of us can connect and achieve the goal of our choice? We all have immense potential to achieve whatever we want in life.

In Swami Vivekananda's words, human souls have infinite potential and can achieve anything. This statement is true but requires wings and a burning desire to achieve what we need to accomplish in life. I have come across many people in my life who were students, professionals, and teachers. I observed that every personality I have interacted with has its routines. Some studying late at night and some waking up early in the morning but then they feel sleepy and inactive the entire day. They were missing the day's power pack. They want to change their habits but somehow they can't. After much of my research on morning waking habits, listening to many podcasts, and reading several books, I concluded that the best way to utilize the morning after waking is first to CHARGE ONESELF WITH A SEQUENCE OF MORNING RITUALS. These morning rituals takes about 60 minutes, and I call this time "Victory Hour".

I have experimented with a series of morning rituals to energize me for the entire day and give me a new outlook for my journey towards becoming an extraordinary person. With my deep learning of morning habits, I desire to write about the morning rituals so that my readers can claim their 'victory hour' and utilize the hour as the best way to charge themselves for the entire day, making them more productive in their work.

## How Did I Come to know About the Morning Rituals?

I was not getting a proper solution to use my morning time efficiently. I was confused as to what time I should wake up. How many hours of sleep I should mandatorily take? If I slept fewer hours, I felt that waking up at the ring of the alarm clock would not freshen up my mind as my body did not get the required hours of sleep. I would snooze my alarm clock button and go back to sleep. Later on, after waking up, I would realize that I had wasted my day again. Further to my frustration of not waking up, I also felt guilty for not sticking to my routine which I had prepared a day before. These routines included walking, reading books, meditating, etc. My thoughts and plan remained on paper, which happened most of the time. It was giving me set back day by day. Still, I was curious to find the real technique of utilizing one hour after waking up in the morning so that I can take on any activity for the entire day. As you read this book, I am sure you will also be going through the same phase, and this happens not only to you but to most of the people who want to become morning people but cannot achieve their goals. I congratulate you for purchasing this book as I can assure you that this dilemma will now be over once and for all. You have purchased this book and reached up to this page, which proves that you want to change your lifestyle and achieve the dreams of your choice. I was always looking for a solution to improve my lifestyle, inculcate good waking habits and utilize the morning hours most beneficially. I had always wanted to be a morning person who ritually sticks to waking up early and feeling energized for the entire day. There was a fire within me to best utilize the morning hours and maintain the consistency of my early waking-up habit. I have researched many books on morning habits to make morning waking a daily ritual. Some books talked about the activities you prefer to be done in the morning based on your liking which may be meditating, reading books, listening to soothing music, running, walking etc. But I was not getting the solution I wanted to kickstart my day. I read many books, listened to many Ted talks on morning habits, and finally, I could merge various concepts after experimenting with various permutations and combinations on me to form a set of morning habits that changed my life. I have been following these morning rituals for the past five years, and I strongly recommend adopting these rituals, which have changed my life.

I have devised strategic time-bound morning activities one after the other for 60 minutes that set the tone for the day. The activities re-energize and revitalize me and make me feel at the top of the world. After my morning activities, I feel highly confident, with all thoughts aligned properly for the entire day. My face gets a radiance with a positive outlook, and I am ready to accept any task for the day. My memory power and my intelligence to grab any subject have improved. In this journey, I have also treasured the secret of learning conceptually any subject which may be strange to me. I will reveal the secret to the entire universe in my next book, which on practising, will lead you to become a learned personality in any subject, a personality which you have never imagined. Yes, I can vouch that the secret is that strong. But to achieve that, you must first become a morning person by practising the techniques taught in this book. I want my readers to achieve their first level of success. I guarantee that you will be a changed person and achieve health, wealth, prosperity, and happiness. I have done it and achieved it, and still, I am achieving more.

The first principle to start the journey is to forget about your past, who you were, and what you did earlier. Every day is a new day, and it starts today. The book "Awaken the Giant Inside," by Anthony Robbins says that you are what you decide now and can transform yourself. The only mantra is to take a "Decision" and then see the changes this decision will bring in your life. People are in the habit of procrastinating, pulling themselves down, and slowly losing their self-confidence. They don't take decisions, and if they do, they don't remain firm. The first key to success is taking decisions, followed by the habit you must stick to in order to witness the fruits of the decision. Research tells us that if any activity is performed for a continuous

21 days, it becomes a habit, and eventually, after 21 days, one starts enjoying the new habit. I guarantee that once you cross 21 days, you cannot live without those habits. I will discuss in the chapters the morning rituals based on habits you must follow for 21 days. After 21 days, you can find the difference. You will be amazed to find yourself improving in all areas in whichever phase of life you are, whether you are a student, a professional, homemaker, a business person etc. This morning ritual is for everyone, and one can easily imbibe it and get a transformed life. You know what? Life is beautiful, and we should enjoy life by taking advantage of the full potential of mind and body. Once you control your mind and body, you can achieve anything extraordinary. So, let's start learning. A learning journey that is going to transform your life forever. Whatever techniques I am going to talk about are not only the techniques I have assimilated from various sources but also, I have experienced them. I will tell you about each technique in detail in the subsequent chapters. I have applied those techniques to myself and found a dramatic change within me. First and foremost, start with your sleeping habits.

## How much sleep is required?

I have researched several articles on the optimum hours of sleep required, but I could not find the answer. Based on the various articles I have read, I did multiple experiments on myself by sleeping early and resting for 7 hours, 8 hours and even for 9 hours. Sleeping to what extent is important is always a question in the mind of everyone. I am sure these thoughts might be going through your thought process as well as how many hours to sleep because many times if you sleep late, you do not feel fresh in the morning. The entire day you feel lazy. But the question is whether this is a roadblock in our minds. Whether our mind should witness 7 or 8 hrs of sleep and only then we can feel fresh in the morning. You will not agree with me now. Once you go through the chapters you will understand the science of feeling energetic. I have interacted with many people and asked how many hours of sleep they need. I get the answer in the range of 7hrs-8hrs, and some even say 9 hrs. But when I ask them, do you feel fresh after waking up? I get a mixed reply. Some say yes, and some say it depends on sleep quality. But then I also ask them if they feel energetic the whole day and have good vibes and thoughts for performing their work in the office or business. Few are sure, but few are unsure of where their life is taking them. They are just flowing wherever life takes them. In the book "Awaken the Giant Inside", Anthony Robbins said that for most people, their life is like a free boat moving in the direction of a stream of water. Wherever the stream is taking the boat, the boat is moving, but at one point, when the sudden steep creeks come, the boat goes along with the water flow and falls into the creek. This is dangerous. Similarly, people take their lives. Their lives move like the boat moving with the flow of a stream. They don't take charge of their life of which they are capable. They can change the direction of their life with just one decision to change their life for the better like using the oars. The direction of the boat can be changed and the boat can be moved to a pleasant place where one can see more greenery and enjoy the surroundings. This example calls for immediate taking control of our life, and each of us can do it.

Life is wonderful, but the only essential is to know the technique of enjoying life. I will tell you how to enjoy life and take full advantage of life. Each one of the readers here is blessed to have a beautiful life. Life of your dreams. A life on your terms. A life of financial freedom. A life of abundance and wealth. A life of good health, and I guarantee that once you follow the techniques given in the book- you will be amazed to find a dramatic improvement in yourself. Yes, you can and have the inherent potential to do that. All the techniques I will discuss in this book are straightforward and do not require spending any amount. It is simply maintaining consistency in your morning ritual habits that you must perform in your Victory Hour. The only commitment I want from you is to follow the Morning Victory Hour habits in true spirit and not miss a day practising those techniques.

Some readers may think they are night owls and can't wake up in the morning. They have been sleeping very late in the night for so many years and will find it hard to suddenly break that chronic habit. The answer is you can with just one decision of waking up early in the morning no matter when you sleep. It is a hard decision, but it will bring you positive results. The following quote of Boxing Champion Muhammad Ali will inspire you **"I hated every minute of training, but I said," Don't quit. Suffer now and live the rest of your life as a champion."**

 One should always take a cue from the universe to lead a beautiful life. The way the universe operates for the entire 24 hours from the rising sun to sunset to night. Similarly, our body is made on certain principles and follows the universe's clock. The universe, if you observe minutely, teaches us a lot. The rising of the sun and the setting of the sun have a fixed time. When the sun rises, a beautiful morning starts with sun rays becoming brighter and brighter, and all living beings are expected to start their day and get busy in their activities. After sunset, the sun's rays slowly dimmer, and the same bright day becomes dark, indicating that living beings should start settling for rest and sleep. Universe has set the timetable of daytime for work and night for sleeping. This is the first principle on which the learnings of this book are based. Some readers might think that because of their office work they have to work late at night and then how do they wake up in the morning? Don't worry. This book is for everyone, and the techniques taught do not impress upon seven or eight hours of sleep. It teaches you to energize yourself for the whole day by practising the laid-down techniques after you wake up. You must "Grab your victory hour" after you wake up and follow the rituals taught in the book to become more productive in your work, achieve your dreams, and succeed in any field you desire. You become extraordinary by practising the techniques for 60 minutes daily. Enjoy your learning journey.

# Chapter 2: Habit

**"Motivation is what gets you started. Habit is what keeps you going."**

**-     Jim Ryun**

Habit is a crucial part of life as without it, consistency is unattainable and consistency is eminent in reaching our success goals. We have beautiful desires in life; to become rich, become famous personalities and so much more but in the end, we cannot catch our dreams because we feel it's impossible and what is presently going on in our lives becomes accepted as our fate but this is not correct. We can become billionaires, popular singers, popular Rockstars, CEO of a billionaire company, the best motivational speaker etc. We undermine ourselves and think that those personalities are different and that we are not even one per cent close to their level. This belief subdues us, and we remain slaves to our poor thoughts. We cannot grow with this thought and we find ourselves adjusting to our present life or rather accept that whatever is happening to us is our fate. Our fate has been predetermined and we cannot do anything. We start settling for less and go with the flow of life. But a study shows that we are what we think. Author Anthony Robbins very well enumerates in his book "Awaken the Giant Inside" that the power of decision can change our life then and there, the moment we decide on something. It is as simple as taking a decision, and we can immediately take a U-turn. We start seeing a change in our life because of that small firm decision which we had been procrastinating.

If we refer to dictionary, we will find the word "Decision" meaning to cut oneself from the ideas holding us back and take a different path altogether on the idea that we think is right and appropriate. We all know what is right or wrong, but the human tendency is such that it always finds its path to the comfort zone and finally settles in that zone. The Comfort zone makes us feel satiated and inhibits us from acting or taking any strain in life. This leads to complacency, and we lose the talent hidden in us. We only look at other people's status, witness their success, see how rich they are, and then make our minds understand that those successful people were born by God's blessing with a silver spoon. We highly regard those people, and they become our ideal. We then mentally settle that good fortune and becoming an ideal personality is not our cup of tea. If we look at the history of rich entrepreneurs like Ambani, Tata etc., we will find that everyone struggled initially; nobody was born rich. They were born with the same physical and mental capabilities as us, but one thing that has made the difference is their mindset. They had that rigid mindset of discipline and punctuality, which made all the difference based on the decision they took then. My question now is, when people who started from scratch can become billionaires, why can't you? Think about it. **"All power is within you; you can do anything and everything"** - these are the lines of Swami Vivekananda. And I have full faith in this one statement of Swami Vivekananda. I have experienced it. Like a common person, I used to be in my comfort zone, watching TV late at night, and waking up late in the morning. Waking up in the morning only to rush to the office to reach on time, nothing remains bright for me because I was flowing with the flow of the office pressure. Similarly, this is true for students and personalities in different professions waking up late in the morning and then rushing to school, office, or business.

A lot of people have the habit of checking emails and WhatsApp messages first thing in the morning once awake.This is unnecessary as you get entangled in social media messages and emails. You loose control of yourself and your life gets directed by others. You lose the kick of the day. The day that you should have owned it is now getting controlled by someone else. Have you ever analyzed why this is happening? The answer to this is not following the morning routine once you wake up. Your morning hour after your wake up is your victory hour, and you need to grab that one hour after you wake up to charge yourself for the entire day. Once you do the morning rituals taught in the book, you will be on top of your energy level for the entire day and feel the difference from day one. Now is when you must change yourself, and while reading this book, you are getting a hint in your subconscious to change yourself. Please follow your inner conscience. It is a one-moment decision, and you must decide to change yourself. There is no other way. Once you have decided that you need to improve your habits, you must remain firm on them. I am telling you that you will be a changed person when you decide to change your habits and adopt a good one. Habit requires discipline and consistency. It is quite human to fall back into your comfort zone when you adopt a good habit. You may be consistent for a few days, but then there is every chance you will return to square one. However, there is a way to come out of it and the way is to be consistent in your mindset of maintaining discipline. The discipline of religiously following the morning rituals taught in this book. Research tells us that anything we practice for 21 days will become our habit, and then after 21 days, we cannot live without those good habits. I have experimented on myself and any day because of exigency if I am unable to perform the morning ritual, I feel a void in my life. Wherever I am, I religiously do my morning ritual. When I read books about morning rituals, I was excited to wake up and set the alarm clock for 5.30 am. When the alarm clock started ringing in the morning, I immediately walked to my alarm clock, dismissed it and was ready to start my morning ritual. The alarm clock should always be kept at a distance so that you can walk and break your sleep pattern. It's a human tendency to go back to your comfort zone. After my first day ritual, I was excited to wake up in the morning the next day but my motivation was a little less on the second day because there was a feeling inside my mind that I had slept less, and I should go to bed and sleep for one more hour. It is effortless to get trapped in the habits we have been following for ages because that doesn't require the inertia for change. We are very much satisfied with the style of life we are living. If we ponder what is holding us back, we will find that we don't want to shift from our comfort zone. It is our inertia of rest which is holding us back. Newton's first law of motion states that a body will remain in the state of rest until and unless an external force is applied. This is true for our human body as well as our comfort zone is our inertia of rest and our decision is the force within us which will compel us to move to an uncomfortable zone. If you are determined to change your habit of waking up early in the morning, you will immediately change yourself to a different personality at that very moment of your decision.

As told earlier, any habit performed continuously for 21 days becomes part of our life, and after 21 days, we enjoy the new habit. When we miss that habit for a day, we get the inner call that we are lacking something in our daily routine and we will not feel 100% for the entire day. So, the first seven days of getting into the good habit are crucial because in this period, we have every chance to fall back on the previous comfort zone from where we started the journey. For not falling back, you need to have a strong mindset of maintaining the consistency of getting into the new habit zone. You must keep yourself calm and believe that you are improving every day by 1% even though those changes will not be much visible to you initially.

In the book "Compound effect", the author says that little changes every day will bring a compound effect on you. This is true. Do not fall prey to your mind renouncing the new habit getting developed in you. The mind has the habit of dragging us to our comfort zone. If you can control your mind for these seven days, I can assure you that you have won the race. This is a difficult period which you must pass through, and it is a known fact that there is every chance for you to slide back to your original place of the journey from *where you started but do not do that. Become conscious of these facts and win over your m*indset. In the next seven days, from the 8th to the 14th day, you will find improvement in yourself. You will feel good and your conscience will tell you that you are becoming a changed person. Here also, a positive feeling of change has come to you, there is every chance of again falling back to your original comfort zone. The simple thumb rule is not to follow your mind.

Follow your intelligence which is above your mind. The mind has the habit of disrupting you, but your intelligence is above the mind to protect you from negative thoughts. Maintain the consistency of the new habit for 14 days. Do not miss a single day; slowly, you will reach your semi-goal post of 14 days journey. Yes, when you have completed your 14 days, I would say, based on my experience that you have acquired 90% of the good habit, and now you are a changed person. People will start looking at you differently, and you will feel proud of your achievement and your decision to transform yourself internally.

Next is the journey from Day 15 to Day 21. This is the honeymoon period, where you will find that you cannot live without performing those habits. There will be an internal call pushing you to perform those habits. This period is the period of urge where you cannot live a single day without those good habits you have developed. Now out of my experience, I can vouch that after this 21 day journey, you will be a changed and transformed person. You will be a different personality altogether. This 21-day activity is the game changer for your life, which is true for any habit you want to develop. Further in my chapters, I want you to build on this 21-day habit. The secret which I am going to tell you is based on this platform which is called "Habit".

# Chapter 3: Exercise

**"I hated every minute of training, but I said," Don't quit. Suffer now and live the rest of your life as a champion."**

**- Muhammad Ali**

**The first morning ritual** in your victory hour is "Exercise". Research shows that each time we wake up our brain is initially slow and less receptive. But then, if aggravated, it does wonders. I have read many books and listened to many podcasts and seminars on morning habits. Every podcast and book teaches and asks you to fix your morning routine to suit you. After doing much research and experimenting on myself, I found that you must first do EXERCISE after you wake up. The best way to exercise is to tune and dance to the music of your choice. Your intention should be to sweat on music. **Researchers have found that aerobic exercise produces endorphins, or "feel good" chemicals. It also increases**

**your heart rate, which triggers norepinephrine, a chemical that helps the brain deal with stress more effectively. Also, exercise helps to increase blood flow to the brain. As you begin exercising, depending on the intensity, a number of important chemical messengers called neurotransmitters are released throughout your nervous system which gives you a positive feeling.**

I have personally experienced that once you dance and jump to music, your heart rate increases, your mind gets alleviated, you feel that your brain is opening, and everything around you looks bright. You will experience a feel-good factor from within. For exercise, you can allocate 15 minutes. Using a timer on your mobile is always best to fix every activity's time slot. I guarantee you will enjoy this activity of dancing to music. If you like walking, you can also go hiking or if running suits, you can run for 15 minutes. The idea is to sweat. This is the first principle for a good start. Further, I will throw more light on other steps one by one.

We often need clarification about what to do after waking up in the morning. There should be a sense of purpose for waking up. The purpose of waking up should be more rewarding than our impulse to go back to sleep for a few hours. I have gone through all the phases of confusion. However, I found that my purpose of performing morning rituals and feeling energetic for the entire day was more rewarding than snoozing my alarm clock and going back to sleep.

## Why do I recommend exercise to be the first morning ritual in your victory hour?

After getting motivated by several Ted talks to wake up early in the morning, I fixed my alarm clock for 5.30 am with a determination to start the day and feel cherished for having woken up early in the morning. My alarm clock used to ring at 5.30 am, but after waking up and putting a few sprinkles of water on my face, I meditated for 10 minutes. I observed that practicing meditation as the first-morning ritual dragged me to a sleepy state. I practiced this because I read in one of the books that we can start our day with meditation, but the first-morning meditation ritual did not give me the required momentum to push forward. My mind was not opening. Next practice, after meditation, I did exercise for 15 minutes. I was astonished that after exercising for 15 minutes, I found a brighter focus in my mind. The blurry images after waking up became sharp. I felt happy and could also feel a good amount of energy syncing. The exercise I selected was dancing to music, where I used to jump slowly on my feet, as my heartbeat also increased. I enjoyed the DJ's music by shaking my body and sweating for 15 minutes. It was a game-changer for me. Everything around me started looking bright, and I felt more focused as if my mind had opened. Mentally and physically, I was feeling fit. A positive feeling, a positive vibe started rushing through my veins. I was feeling blessed. This feeling left me with an altogether different experience and provoked me to change the sequence of my morning rituals after waking up. The following day, I was very excited to wake up at 5.30 am with a thought to start my day by dancing to the music of my choice. What a bright idea! It served the twin purpose of dancing to the tune of my favorite music, enjoying it, and simultaneously accomplishing the benefits of morning exercise sweating profusely. I was so happy with this accomplishment that I felt as if I had conquered the world. My 40 years of confusion about how to make my morning bright got an apt solution. I was excited and eager to experiment on whether I could make Exercise my first-morning ritual. If yes, it could be a game changer.

With good thought, I slept that night and as usual, I woke up at 5.30 am ready for the experiment. After drinking a glass of lukewarm water, I immediately went to the living room, where I kept everything ready, like my ear pod, my favorite DJ music tuned on my mobile, and sports shoes. I set a timer of 15 minutes on my mobile and then turned on the music of my choice. The first track of the music of my favorite song in my ear gave me a serene and elated feeling. My feet started throbbing to the tune, and my body slowly started shaking to the theme of the music. Slowly and slowly, I went deep into the music; there was a smile on my face, and I was excited about the music being played. I was jumping, dancing, and shaking my body to the tune of the music. I was enjoying the music and sweating. My mind was becoming more apparent, and I could feel that my mind was opening and everything in and around the surrounding started to look brighter. I was feeling more accomplished. There was much energy in me. I cherished the moment and felt blessed from the inside. There was a feeling that others were sleeping and yet to start the day. I had already started and was ready to take charge for the day. It was 5.50 am, and I finished my first-morning ritual. It was a crushing victory for me.

Simply a little warm-up, dancing to the music, and jumping off the ground will sweat you and increase your heartbeat which is very good for your health. I recommend the first-morning ritual to do exercise, which can  sweat you. I guarantee that you will feel the difference after 15 minutes of exercise. First, drink a glass of lukewarm water as it instantly energizes you after a gap of 6-7 hours of sleep. It keeps your body hydrated during exercise.

# Chapter 4: Breathing Exercise

"Whenever your mind becomes scattered, use your breath as the means to take hold of your mind again "

-Thich Nhat Hanh

**The second morning ritual** in your victory hour is the "Breathing Exercise". It is a known fact that no living being can exist without breath. We exist because we can breathe. My question is- have we recognized the importance of breath or are we conscious of the breath we take in and take out? Unfortunately, we don't as it happens naturally, and why should we bother about what happens naturally? Everyone thinks that way.

Breathing is a subconscious function. When we sleep at night, our breathing continues because breath is our friend and will always remain with us. But what if we devote some time to feel our breath and also realize the importance of breath and further leverage it to improve our life? For this, I suggest a "breathing exercise" to be done every day for 5 minutes. The technique is to sit in a quiet place with your back straight and start inhaling and exhaling the air peacefully with a conscious mind.

You can either sit with your legs crossed or on a chair, whatever suits you. You have to place your right thumb on the right nostril and inhale air deeply from the left nostril. Hold your breath for a few seconds and then place your right middle finger on the left nostril and then exhale the air out from the right nostril. Next, with your right middle finger placed on the left nostril, inhale the air deeply from the right nostril. Hold it for a few seconds and then by placing the right thumb on the right nostril, you can exhale the air from the left nostril. This breathing in and breathing out exercise is one cycle and you can repeat the cycle ten times. You will feel the soothing vibration in your mind. It will bring calmness within you. I have been practising this breathing exercise for the last five years, giving immense energy from within, and much clarity of thoughts. You will have a feeling of purity after performing this exercise.

There are also other health benefits associated with practising this breathing exercise. This breathing exercise is called **Pranayama**. Pranayama is the practice of breath regulation. It's a main component of yoga, an exercise for physical and mental wellness. You purposely inhale, exhale and hold your breath in a specific sequence. Pranayama is an ancient practice of controlling your breath. You control the timing, duration and frequency of every breath and hold. The goal of pranayama is to connect your body and mind. It also supplies your body with oxygen while removing toxins. This is meant to provide physiological healing benefits.

## Research Done

A Research paper based on a study conducted on 50 adults subject to know the effect of pranayama over a period of 6 weeks, suggested the following results.

1. It strengthens your lungs
2. It acts as a stress reliever
3. Improves concentration
4. Improves sleep quality
5. Boost immunity
6. Improves cardiovascular health
7. Improves Digestion
8. Glows skin

The benefits of this breathing exercise are immense. Please make it a part of your morning ritual so that you become both mentally and physically strong.

Reference: <u>12 Benefits of Pranayama (Yoga Breathing) for Body and Brain - Fitsri</u>

# Chapter 5: Affirmation

**"I promise myself to be so strong that nothing can disturb my peace of mind."**

**- Christian D. Larson**

**The third morning ritual** in the victory hour is "Affirmation". Many readers may not understand the exact meaning of this word. What exactly is Affirmation?  After reading several articles on affirmation and listening to a lot of podcasts, I could deeply understand the meaning of affirmation. Affirmation is made from the word "affirm", which means that you believe something is true and you strongly support it. More than that, there is a big YES to it from your side. If you can apply those thoughts in your daily life, I can vouch that your dreams or the person you want to become will become true. Yes, you rightly listened. You must believe and tell your mind that you are the person whom the world wants to see as a great personality.

As a reader, you might dream of becoming a company's successful CEO, entrepreneur, homemaker, bright student, and reaching any height in your dream career. The list is endless. You can achieve whatever you want through affirmations. Mike Tyson used to affirm daily that he was the no. 1 champion in Boxing. Every day repeating these words rewired his mind, and his brain started believing it. He became the world champion in Boxing. This is true for anyone. If you are a professional and want to be the best in your field, you can affirm daily that you are your organization's shining star and the best employee. In affirmation, you must continuously say the positive thoughts from your heart that you want to achieve. You have to say it aloud as if you have already achieved it. You must train your mind and brain to believe that you are on the path to achieving your thoughts and that those thoughts are now your life's real situation.

Research shows that the human brain encounters 60, 000 thoughts a day and many thoughts pull you down and land you in the past. You get trapped in those thoughts. Those thoughts generate feelings of loneliness, and you start reacting low. On the contrary, if you feel good, your thoughts becomes good and you have a positive outlook. Your feelings send a frequency to the universe and bring back the same emotions so that your feeling continues in whatever state you are in. If you feel sad, you send the low frequency to the universe. The universe will bring some sad images and thoughts in front of your eyes and make you feel sad. Further sad events may also happen, and make you feel depressed. On the contrary, if you feel good and send the positive frequency to the universe, the universe will bring more positive feelings and events into your life to make you remain in that positive state. This is the secret of life, and the law of attraction has been discussed in detail in the book "Secret".

Affirmations are positive feelings of achievement you send to the universe. When you program your mind every day for 5 minutes in the morning hours, you are sending positive vibes to the universe. The universe in return, brings you more of such events which makes you happier and gives a sense of positive feeling. Slowly, you start attracting the positive events for the affirming thoughts of your mind and you will find that the thoughts you always send as an affirmation daily becomes a reality. You become the person of your choice.

 Affirmation plays a vital role in the life of successful people. If you read the biography of successful people, you will be amazed to know that successful people continuously send positive affirmations to the universe. In return they get positive vibes from the universe and achieve success daily. Daily affirmations for 5 minutes in the morning hours will bring a sea change in you and bring you close to the dreams of your choice. You will encounter your dream, which will be a reality for you. This is the power of affirmation. Science says that when you affirm, your brain gets programmed in that direction and starts creating positive thoughts, which brings you a good feeling. You emit a positive frequency in the universe, and in return, you attract a positive frequency from the universe through positive events associated with the dream. You start getting opportunities associated with your daily affirmation, and the situation becomes congenial for you day by day. Your mind and body gets wired toward the success you want and then achieve it. But in the end, I repeatedly say that consistency is king. You must do this affirmation exercise every day for 5 minutes, and the results will be pronounced. If followed diligently, I guarantee that the morning victory hours routine will lead you to change your personality. You will find a new person in you after a few weeks of practice of the morning routine. I have done, and I have found the changes in me. I have also read and learnt from other books, and I applied them to me and it worked for me. I want readers to practice it and then proliferate the concept of morning rituals so that the world becomes a much better place to live in and every human being in this universe becomes happy and starts enjoying the universe.

**Research shows that there is MRI evidence suggesting that certain neural pathways are increased when people practice self-affirmation tasks (Cascio et al.,1516). If you want to be super specific, the ventromedial prefrontal cortex- involved in positive valuation and self-related information processing -becomes more active when we consider our personal values (Falk et al.,1515; Cascio et al.,1516).**

To conclude, I would like to quote the stanza from the book "Secret" wherein the author gave an example of Genie where you rub the vessel and the Genie appears asking for the command to be followed. He says, "Your wish is my command". Similarly, we all human beings must wish and the universe must obey the command. You are the master of the universe. Belief is essential; once your affirmations have commanded you, you need to believe persistently and the results will be in front of you. Never doubt your belief. The Universe will bring the result as you think. If you suspect, the universe will give mixed results. Like when you visit a restaurant and give an order, you don't think about the food getting prepared. You believe that whatever you have ordered will be delivered to you. You don't go on asking and doubting the waiter for the order. Similar is our thought. Once we fix on the goal we want to achieve, we affirm ourselves. Make your mind believe that you are already performing it and your dreams are getting prepared in the universe, like the food getting prepared in the restaurant you ordered. Your order must come. This is the truth.

Practice affirmation every day for 5 minutes as one of the morning victory hour rituals to become an extraordinary person.

# Chapter 6: Visualization

**"To bring anything into your life, imagine it's already there."**

**-Richard Bach**

**The fourth morning ritual** in your victory hour is "visualization". Visualization is an ancient technique practiced by many successful people in the universe. This technique is suggested in your morning routine because practising it helps you to become the person of your dreams and this dream can be turned into reality. This technique is also called the law of attraction. You attract dreams inspired by your thoughts. I will tell you in detail how to practice this technique.

By learning, you will slowly realize that the universe is bringing the things you wanted in your life. Opportunities start coming to you and you start taking benefits of that. You become part of those opportunities and immediately start acknowledging the opportunity. You will experience that you have been waiting for this miracle to happen and suddenly, things will start moving in your desired direction. This works always and has worked for thousands of people.

In 1954, Roger Bannister, an athlete, decided to run 1 mile in 4 minutes. He was told that this was an impossible idea that was cropping into his mind. But Roger Bannister did not believe in other people's mindsets. Also, the town's physicians said it was humanly impossible to run 1 mile in 4 minutes. Roger Bannister was determined to break the myth of all the people around him. He started visualizing the entire event of running and started practising every day. He visualized his victory every day and clearly heard the clapping sound of his victory from the audience. He saw the entire event of victory in his mind not once but several times, and when D-day came, it was to the surprise of everyone that he broke the record and ran 1 mile in less than 4 minutes. After that, many athletes broke the record of running 1 mile in less than 4 minutes. This is the power of visualization. **Many scientific studies have proven that mental training with visualization is an effective strategy for many forms of athletics, from throwing darts and basketball to sprinting and weight training,**

**to Olympic competitions. Olympic athletes from various disciplines, including gymnastics, diving, judo, and fencing, use visualization to prepare for competition.**

In his book "Awaken the Giant Inside", Anthony Robbins gives the example of Mike Tyson. Mike Tyson wanted to become the best boxer in the world and be accoladed as the number one boxer. He followed the principle of visualization. Every day he visualized that he was the best boxer in the world and was getting victories after victories and he was winning medals. He clearly saw that he was crushing other opponent players and was declared champion. And today, we can witness Mike Tyson becoming the champion in Boxing. His dream turned into reality. Many successful people have realized this power of attraction. They started practising visualization in their daily work. Slowly, they found that things began working as expected and they became successful day by day.

Definitely, at this point, you might be inquisitive to know how visualization works and how you can follow the steps of visualization so that you can experiment with yourself to become the person of your choice and improve further in your life. Everyone wants to improve and achieve success in their life in whichever phase of life they are in. We often try to achieve our dream but later feel that those dreams are not achievable, and we compromise with the weakening thoughts coming into our minds and we settle for less. We get satiated by the flow of life and don't adventure further to achieve the dreams of our choice.

I have read many articles on visualization and wanted to test the technique by following the steps for visualization. I practised that and found an utter surprise when the goal I dreamt of started coming to me as an opportunity which I believe to be a ladder for success and achieving my dream. I started every day by visualizing writing a book on Motivation that is helping my readers to improve their lives, and today the result is in front of you. Yes, it works. Visualization is one of your daily routine rituals and should be followed arduously daily. As a reader, you might have varied dreams, some of you want to become a successful professional, a successful CEO, a good homemaker, a motivational speaker, a best-seller author etc., and the list continues. Visualization can bring success to anyone.

Whatever dream you have in your mind and the thought of making that dream true should always be at the top of your mind. For visualization, you must devote 5 minutes to the morning ritual hour. The dream you want to achieve should be visible to you as if you have already achieved the dream. Let us say you want to be successful in the interview and get promoted. Then you need to visualize the process you are following to get promoted. You visualize that you are reading so many articles about the questions to be asked in the interview. You visualize the day before your interview. You visualize that you are fully prepared and have a peaceful sleep before your interview. The next morning you are getting ready for the interview. All dress is well arranged, and you also see the color of the shirt, trouser, tie, blazer etc. You must feel the entire process as if it is happening to you. Then see clearly how you are travelling on the interview day and sitting in the waiting room with other candidates for your interview turn. Feel the confidence on your face. See the candidate coming out of the interview room, and then your turn comes for interview. Visualize clearly how you are knocking on the door and sitting on the chair. See the interview members, the questions each member asks, and how confidently you are answering the question with a smile on your face. See clearly that all the interview members are happy with your knowledge, and everyone is impressed. The interview members are feeling satisfied as if you were the candidate they were looking for. See clearly that they are saying to you – Best of luck, and with humbleness, you thank them and come out of the interview room. You feel the joy on your face, and then you visualize that you got selected for the interview and got the offer letter. This is one of the examples I have given to make you understand the concept of visualization. The same mental journey can be for any dream you want to achieve. Your thoughts in a positive direction are bound to attract the positiveness and will give you success. The crux is that you must experience the feeling of success in your visualization journey.

Visualization has the power to make yourself familiar with the situation you are going to encounter. You can apply this technique to any activity you want to achieve. Suppose you have to give a presentation to your boss or client, you can visualize the entire proceedings of the presentation in your mind, you can see everyone in the conference room giving you thumbs-up for the wonderful presentation. Practice it and you will feel fulfilled even before you grab success. You will feel that you are encountering a real situation. The actual event which will occur will be your second victory. The first victory was already by you won in your mind. From today onwards, set aside five minutes for the visualization process. This is one of the morning rituals in your victory hour. Practice it daily, and you will see the difference in your life and find yourself much ahead towards your journey of becoming an extraordinary person.

# Chapter 7: Meditation

**"Calmness of mind is one of the beautiful jewels of wisdom".**

**-James Allen**

**The fifth morning ritual** in your victory hour is "Meditation". The mind has the habit of wandering here and there, but Meditation, which is the fifth Morning ritual can solve the wavering slides of the mind. You might have heard and read much about meditation but for me, meditation simply means pure silence of the mind. It is essential to calm our minds because often times, the mind drifts so far away from the positivity it should actually focus on. That is why it is called "Monkey Mind". Monkey has the habit of jumping from one tree branch to another. They are never at peace and keep doing things here and there. The mind can be compared to it. It is never stable and keeps wandering. You might have often experienced that your thoughts takes you to your past days when you were sad or something unpleasant happened to you and you keep thinking about those events. This thought process makes you feel gloomy. The mind tends to fall back to the past and bring to you the events that occurred and you get trapped in those thoughts. This is true for everyone. But is there a way out to keep control of our minds? Can we mould our minds as we want? Can we mould our minds to think only positive thoughts? Yes, these all are possible.

**Research has confirmed the beneficial aspects of meditation. In addition to having better focus and control over their emotions, many people who meditate regularly have reduced levels of stress and bolstered immune systems. In a study published in the journal "NeuroImage", researchers report that certain regions in the brains of long-term meditators were larger than in a similar control group. Specifically, meditators showed significantly larger volumes of the hippocampus and areas within the orbitofrontal cortex, the thalamus and the inferior temporal gyrus- all regions known for regulating emotions.**

The Bhagwat Gita mentions that the mind is just above the senses. Rather the sequence is; senses are subordinate to the mind, the mind is subordinate to Intelligence, and Intelligence is subordinate to the soul, i.e., our inner self. The five senses; the ears, eyes, nose, tongue, and touch, can disrupt us if we do not take care of these senses. The mind can easily get carried away by the senses. Let us understand with an example. You might have experienced that when it comes to eating ice cream, burgers etc. your mind immediately responds positively. We cannot control our feelings and get into the act of eating ice cream and burgers. Here our sense organ the tongue, plays the game and incites our minds to enjoy the food. We get carried by our minds as the senses ignite the desire to eat ice cream and burgers. This is true for any activity about our senses, where our senses invigorate us to do things, and our mind gets readily in sync with our senses. Our acts become what our mind says, and this becomes the beginning of our personality making us judged by others through our acts. We get carried away by our minds and we justify to ourselves that the activity we are going to do is right. If we feel guilty about our actions, our mind convinces us that we can correct ourselves later or find another alternative to balance the action we have taken. But it never happens, and we get into the trap of senses and mind. I am telling you all these because we should always understand how our body and mind works. We can only correct our mind's strengths and weaknesses if we know them in depth.

Going further above the mind is intelligence. Now, this is very important because our mind has the habit of getting carried away by the senses, but then our intelligence should control our mind. Intelligence can understand what is right or wrong and for any action our mind says to perform, our intelligence should be able to judge it and convey to our mind whether to do it or not. Often our sense of taste will provoke us to eat ice cream, and based on that provocation, our mind agrees with our senses and we are ready for action. But here comes the "Intelligence", which controls the mind and says "No"- eating ice cream is not good for your health, and you should not eat it. You take the immediate decision not to eat, so your mind gets controlled. Now, who controlled your mind?

It is your intelligence. Intelligence judges what is right or wrong and accordingly gives instructions to the mind. Your intelligence will make you a learned personality and a person of good character. And finally above intelligence, is our soul, which is as pure as a crystal and has the power to get connected to God. Connecting to your inner self or soul is spiritual. I am telling you all these things to help you realize that when we were born, we were at peace and enjoyed every moment. As newborn babies, we had tranquillity in our minds and were happy with our toys or whatever was given to us. That is the pure state of mind. But as we grew, we gathered many experiences in our lives, attached emotions to our various experiences and slowly lost the calmness of our mind. We easily get disturbed, which is true for many of us in whichever phase of life we are in. The solution for getting us back to our original pure state of mind is the devotion of just 5 minutes daily for Meditation.

So, my fifth-morning ritual is Mediation. When I say meditation, it means keeping your mind silent for 5 minutes. Practice this every day, and you will find a sea change in you. You will find calmness in your mind and clarity in your thoughts. You will feel energized. As I said, practicing just 5 minutes of silence daily will significantly change your personality if you maintain consistency. You might now be eager to know the techniques for mediation and why I am recommending mediation for just 5 minutes. I will guide you on how best to utilize those 5 minutes of your precious time and get the best advantage. I have read many books on meditation on different meditation techniques. When I experimented with myself, the best technique that could affect my inner self was closing my eyes and concentrating on my breath. This is the only mantra that will shift your mind from thoughts going through your mind to concentrating on your breathing. The main purpose of mediation is to control your mind. I told you in the previous chapter about the concept of the Monkey mind. Your mind keeps wandering here and there, but when you try to fix your mind on any activity, it will slowly become calm and do what you want. It comes under your control. This is called the power of concentration. Practicing this daily activity will give you a different view of the world you have been experiencing to date.

In the meditation process, sit with your spinal cord straight, close your eyes and concentrate on your breath. Feel the breath you are inhaling and exhaling while keeping your eyes closed. You will initially experience difficulty concentrating on your breath and sitting even for one minute becomes very tiring. But don't worry. It happens initially for everyone. Slowly and slowly, you will get used to it. While meditating, you will initially experience different thoughts visiting your mind, and you get carried by those thoughts.? But it's quite natural. The only technique for such wandering thoughts is to accept them and let them go. Imagine thoughts as clouds and let those clouds of thoughts flow away. Don't get attached to the thoughts. Thoughts will come and go like clouds. But your focus should be on breathing. Feel how your belly rises and gets inside with every breath you take in and take out. Just concentrate on your breathing during these 5 minutes. I assure you that if you practice this technique consistently for 5 minutes, you will gain a lot. You will find the difference in you. Life will look different to you. The same problem which was disturbing will now find a solution. You will start enjoying your life. You will attract all happiness and wealth and slowly find a radiance in your face. Experience it. At whatever age of your life, you are now, you can meditate by either sitting with your crossed legs, keeping your spinal cord straight or if cross-leg sitting doesn't suit you, you can sit on a chair with your back straight and concentrate on your breath. Find a peaceful location in your house and practice it daily for just 5 minutes. To conclude this chapter on mediation, I would bring lines from Bhagat Gita, which says "our five senses are like the five horses pulling the chariot; the chariot is our mind which gets pulled by our senses and the chariot's driver is our intelligence which controls the senses and mind."

In a nutshell, I want to tell you that with the practice of meditation, you will be able to control your mind and break the habit of mind wandering here and there and keeping you trapped in various thoughts. With meditation, you can pull the mind to one thought and slowly, you will find that you have won over your mind. Just as the magnifying glass has the power to burn paper when sun rays are concentrated on it, in a similar way when we learn to concentrate our mind through meditation we can do wonders.  I can guarantee you that there can be no victory for you which can be as powerful as getting control of your mind. Once you control it, situations in your life cannot distract you. You will know how to tackle any situation in your life whatever it may be. Good luck.

# Chapter:8 Reading

**"Reading is a conversation. All books talk. But a good book listens as well."**

-

**Mark Haddon**

**The sixth morning ritual** in your victory hour is "Reading". Reading is very important in life, and when I say reading, I mean reading motivational or self-help books in the morning for 10 minutes. Reading books will charge you and set the tone for the day with positive thoughts in your mind. I have personally experienced this, and I can assure you that positive vibes will be set in your mind, and you will start optimistically looking at life. Again, I would say it is a habit, and habit takes 21 days to recede in you fully. Start reading any motivational book and try to read the book for at least 10 minutes every day as a ritual after you have completed your meditation process. Do not worry about the number of pages you have read in 10 minutes. Initially, for 10 minutes, you may read 1 page or a maximum of 2 pages, but whatever you read, read with full concentration, and try to understand what the author wants to say. I would say books are the one on one communication in which the author is conversing with you. You will feel the thought process of the author. Books are written with many experiences of the author, and the author brings in many research ideas from various sources. Try to absorb yourself in the book, and slowly imbibe the good habits or thoughts talked about in the book. I assure you that you will feel empowered reading self-help books in the morning. You can purchase any motivational book and start reading. Maintain consistency of 10 minutes of reading every day, and slowly you will find the compound effect of completing the book in a few days. But whatever book you purchase, finish it to the end. You should purchase another book only when you have completed the book or feel satisfied with the concepts in the book.

Research shows that 85% of all readers read only the first 10-11 Pages of the book and then leave it. This is not correct, and it is not the correct way of reading. I started reading self-help books for 10 minutes every day after completing my meditation ritual and so far, I have completed reading forty motivational books. It is impressive to have new learning every day with fresh thoughts from the book. From my experience, I will tell you that you will start developing an interest in reading self-help books, and a situation will come when your hobby becomes reading. This stage of developing reading as a hobby is a victory for you. You will become a changed person. You will have a positive outlook on life and in any situation, you will have the wisdom of what is right or wrong. It is well said, "Books are your best friend." Books like friends are always ready to accompany you in sorrow and joy. They motivate you and help you to realize your goal. While reading books, keep a pencil or pen in your hand and mark the important concepts talked about in the book so that you can revisit them whenever you feel you require that punch. Readers are generally shy about marking or writing anything in the new book they have purchased. I also had this feeling initially, but then changed my habit of keeping my book clean after receiving inputs from many authors.

I have a deep gratitude for author Hal Elrod because I learnt a lot from him by reading his books. Books have the power to turn your life. You never know which one line of the book can impact your mind, and it indeed does. Out of my experience, I had always had a deep desire to utilize the morning hour as I was forced to wake up at 4.30 am in childhood. Still, as I said earlier, I was looking for the best methodology for utilizing the morning hours. I started reading many books and listening to many podcasts but could not get the answer. Finally, after reading so many self-help books, I could assimilate the sequence of techniques of morning rituals which can become a power pack energy stimulator for me. Every person has his taste in reading; my taste was in morning habits. But for you, it may be self-help books on mindset, leadership, Intelligence, team building etc. But my only appeal is to start imbibing the habit of reading self-help books. I inculcated the habit of reading books to such an extent that whenever I get free time, I read books. Even if I travel to the office by car, I utilize my time reading self-help books. There will always be a book in the back seat of my car, which I will read whenever I get time. Even if I am onboarded on a flight or waiting in the airport lounge, I will utilize my waiting time to read self-help books. I always have a burning desire to finish the book fast and reward myself instantly by purchasing another book of my choice. Many of my book collections are the books I have purchased at the airport, as that is the best time to go through the summary contents of the book. When I go to a shopping mall with my family, I love to spend 15- 15 minutes at bookstores, where I scan the books of my choice by going through the pages and keeping a note of the name of the books which I like to reward myself later. It is a very nice journey; only experience will tell you how sweet it is, amazing thoughts and amazing ideas, and you start becoming a learned person day by day. Today, when I present this book to you, it is only because of the habit I developed of reading self-help books. So much learning has come in me that now I want to share with the world my experiences which I learned through books. I experimented on myself, added certain things which suited me and then presented to the world from which the world could benefit. You can also do the same. I have learned from Author Anthony Robbins that "One should not spend time reinventing the wheels". If someone has developed certain techniques that worked for him, it should work for others too. You can learn many qualities when you read books on successful personalities. Successful people follow certain disciplines in life; they are today the most respected personalities in society. When they can be a Billionaire, with loads of good health and happiness - why can't you? God has given everyone the same physical features. It is only how we utilize our inherent potential and set boundaries of self-discipline. Reading self-help books in the morning will give you new proactive thoughts daily. You will feel empowered. Try to imbibe the new learnings, and you can reach the next level in your career and become a different personality altogether. I would say the only mantra is maintaining consistency in your activity. 1% improvement every day will make you reach 100% one day. I am sure that reading books will give you a direction in your life, and you will always find a trusted mentor ready to help you in any situation.

Reading books will always calm your mind. Purchase a book marker and keep a bookmarker on the page you have read for that day. This will help you to start your reading journey the next morning from your last read page. For convenience, you can set the timer on your mobile and fix the alarm for 10 minutes. When the mobile alarm snoozes, stop where you are reading and then with the pencil or pen, mark a spot on that line so that the next morning you can start exactly from that line. It helps you become disciplined and brings an inquisitiveness to read what is next for another beautiful morning. Enjoy reading and become a learned personality.

# Chapter 9: Free writing

**"The starting point of discovering who you are, your gifts, talents, and dreams is being comfortable with yourself. Spend time alone. Write in a journal. Take long walks in the woods."**

**-Robin S Sharma**

**The seventh morning ritual** in your victory is "Free Writing". It has the tremendous power to turn you into a positive mindset personality and you begin connecting with yourself. I have read many self-help books and listened to various podcasts on morning writing, but I could not figure out what and when to write in the morning. But out of my practice and then rechanging my sequence of rituals, I found that free writing is most suitable when I finish my other morning victory rituals in the sequence of sweating exercise, breathing exercise, affirmation, visualization, meditation, reading and then free writing. I call it free writing because you write whatever comes to your mind. It may be your emotions or an event that occurred in your life. But 5 minutes of daily free writing will make you a changed person. When it comes to writing, I have had my experience writing in a notebook daily with dates. Writing with dates will help you to make yourself accountable in your daily writing ritual. Just write whatever comes to your mind, and don't worry about grammatical or spelling mistakes. Everything cannot be perfect on the same day. Besides, it's neither an essay competition nor the article you are writing for any newspaper or magazine. You are writing your thoughts which are coming from your mind. And the most important is flow in writing. Just keep on writing for 10 minutes. I can guarantee you that, slowly, you will find that you are getting time to talk to the person you have never talked to "You." Research shows that writing frees up the mind as you write, your mind gets decluttered, and you feel relaxed.

At this moment, while you are reading this page, make up your mind to write every day for ten minutes about any idea that comes to mind. I will give a few examples to clarify: you can write about your achievement for waking up in the morning and following all the morning victory hour rituals. You can also write about the book you read 10 minutes back and what good learning you had from the book. You can also write about what is good in your life, your dream, and what you want to achieve in life. Writing is communicating with oneself. You are expressing your thoughts on a paper which otherwise always revolves in your mind. My experience with writing is that I write 3-4 pages in 5 minutes. I have more than 50 notebooks written as a part of my daily free-writing habits.

I have personally experienced that the beauty of daily writing is that when you are at your leisure, you can go through what you have written and after a gap of let's say, one month, you will be surprised to know that you have learned so many new ideas. This writing habit will one day provoke you to write books, as today I am presenting this book to you, which is a motivation from my daily writing habits. I never thought I would be an author and present my experiences to the universe in the form of this book. This book is my compilation and experiences of the learning I have gathered from various self-help books and podcasts, which I have learned and experimented on. When it has worked on me for the last five years, I wanted to present my learnings to the Universe. Every victory morning ritual talked about in this book, if followed diligently, will make you a guaranteed changed personality. You can gain anything in your life. You can achieve your dreams. You can become a Billionaire. You can have the best of health and the best of happiness in the world. This is why I call the morning hour after you wake up your "Victory hour". The rituals followed diligently will lead you to the dreams of your choice, and guarantee you being a changed person.You have reached up to this page itself speaks aloud that you have high dreams in your life and want to be a changed personality.

Whatever position you are in your life, as a student, homemaker, professional, sportsperson etc., you are bound to change your personality further. Writing your thoughts comes from the right portion of your brain designed to be creative. You are writing from your creative mind and penning down your thought process. In my last five years, I have read many self-help books, spiritual books like Bhagwat Gita, works of Swami

Vivekananda, and watched many motivational movies. Research shows that whatever you read, listen and watch, it keeps on assimilating in your subconscious mind and then you can pen down the learnings. When I go through the 50 notebooks I have written on varied topics- good leadership, learnings from Bhagwat Gita, learning from watching motivational movies, learnings from various Ted talks and podcasts on morning habits, it gives an awesome feeling. Writing should not be restricted only to learning from reading motivational books. It should also expand to your feelings for this world and the beautiful greenery you see around you every day. If you are excited about anything, write down your feelings. You can write about the events which are going to happen for you if you can visualize them. You can write about the presentation you will make today to your client or to your seniors in your office. That is why I say it is free writing. Inculcate the habit which is already within you. Only you need to open yourself and write in a notebook. When I read about this morning's writing ritual, I had a really great feeling inside me to express myself which I was previously unaware of.

Sometimes you need to follow someone if that person has gotten success out of it. It would be best not to put logic in it but rather follow the teachings blindly. I diligently write every day for 10 minutes during my victory hour. I would suggest write anything, even if you feel like not writing. Slowly you will find that when your pen starts running on paper, you start attracting thoughts and your writing flow increases. But keep a pause of 5 minutes by setting alarm snooze on your mobile. I use my mobile to fix each activity's intervals for my morning ritual. It works.

When you complete reading this book, purchase a notebook and a pen with a good grip. For many readers, writing with a pen may be a new journey after graduation. Take this as a challenge and start doing it. You will feel uncomfortable writing for the initial days but don't lose track. Every day a bit of practice will eventually make you write freely. You will initially be able to write only 4-5 sentences for a few days, but that is still good progress. It is not the number of pages you are writing, but as a ritual, you are writing your heart on a piece of paper. Your thoughts which you cannot see, now you can see physically written. It's a great feeling to see your thoughts written on paper. When I first read about this habit of free writing, I felt very excited and immediately went to my nearby shop and purchased a long notebook and a good quality pen with a good grip. In the initial days, I found difficulty writing as I remember I last wrote pages during my post-graduation days when I was pursuing MBA. After a gap of 18 years, I started writing. But slowly, it worked, and I started enjoying writing. For a month, I remember I could write only 1-2 paragraphs but slowly, my writing flow increased with the flow of my thoughts. I experienced that free writing is directly connected to the flow of the mind. At one point, your mind and pen will be in sync. You start producing the thoughts and find the same getting crafted in your notebook. It's an awesome journey. I strongly recommend experiencing this journey of free writing. You will be a changed personality. I can guarantee you.

# Chapter 10: Plan Your Day

"A goal without an action plan is a daydream"

-Nathaniel Branden

**The eighth morning ritual** in your victory hour is "Planning your day". The path to becoming an extraordinary person starts with a strategic planning. If your planning is good, you will be the king in your area of operation. But to reach this planning mindset, your brain has to work at it's full horsepower and this is only possible when you religiously follow the morning rituals taught in this book. From Exercise to free writing in your victory hour and then finally planning your day. We require planning to make our day bright in whatever phase of life we are in. Whether you're a student, professional, businessman, CEO of a company etc., you need to have proper planning to start the day so that everything gets aligned as per your expectation for the day. You will have immense power within you to start your day because you are prepared for what is essential and what to execute.

Planning doesn't mean all the work under the universe should be planned on the same day but rather, it means that the most important tasks should be tackled. The most important lesson that needs your attention should be prioritized. In the book by Brian Tracy, "Eat that Frog", the author talks about eating first the ugliest frog in the morning, as after eating the ugliest frog, one can eat any frog. Here, the ugliest frog means the work that is very important and cannot be procrastinated. Once you eat the ugliest frog, all other work will seem accomplished or will seem to be very easy.

There was once a businessman looking for advice to run the business and earn much profit. A town consultant approached him with the offer to help him. However, the consultant's demand was first to be handed over, 10 million dollars before he would hand over a sealed envelope to the businessman with the solution there. Also, the consultant told the businessman that he would return the money if he didn't like the solution. The businessman agreed with the offer of consultant. As promised, the businessman paid 10 million dollars to the consultant after receipt of the sealed envelope. The businessman opened the sealed envelope. There was a white piece of paper inside the envelope and on it was just one sentence "Write five important works you want to do today and stick to it". Reading this line, the businessman had a smile on his face, and he agreed to part with the money and thanked the consultant for opening his eyes. He thanked him that the solution was worth more than 10 million dollars.

In the morning victory hour, I strongly recommend meticulously planning your day by devoting 10 minutes. Close your eyes and think of the task at hand and jot down on a piece of paper, the topmost important works to be done for the day. Stick to your plan. Practising this habit on a daily basis will lead you to become productive in your work and you will own the day.

# Morning Rituals in sequence at a glance:
## <u>(Strictly follow in this order)</u>

| No Morning ritual | Morning Ritual | Time Duration |
| --- | --- | --- |
| 01. | Exercise | 15 minutes |
| 02. | Breathing Exercise | 5 minutes |
| 03. | Affirmation | 5 minutes |
| 04. | Visualization | 5 minutes |
| 05. | Meditation | 5 minutes |
| 06. | Reading | 10 minutes |
| 07. | Free Writing | 5 minutes |
| 08. | Planning your day | 10 minutes |
| **Total time duration** | | **60 minutes** |

# Acknowledgements

I thank my parents who have inculcated in me, a good habit of reading books thereby making this book compilation to you possible. I am highly indebted to my wife, Sanchita, who always encouraged me to write the learnings I  practice, by listening to various podcasts and reading self-help books for the betterment of the readers. This book would not have been possible without her support and the sacrifices she made on weekends allowing me to write the book. I would also like to acknowledge the sacrifice made by my little daughter, Ishanvi as she did not demand playing with me whenever she found me writing the manuscript. I love both of them

Copyright © 1522 by Gyan S Narayan.  All rights reserved. No part of this book may be reproduced in any form without permission in writing from the author. No part of this publication may be reproduced or transmitted in any form or by any means, mechanical or electronic, including photocopying or recording, or by any information storage and retrieval system, or transmitted by email or by any other means whatsoever without permission in writing from the author.

www.ingramcontent.com/pod-product-compliance
Lightning Source LLC
Chambersburg PA
CBHW071214260726
48653CB00041B/754